DEBUSSY

IMAGES

for Orchestra
No. 2 Ibéria
Edited by / Herausgegeben von
Roger Fiske

Ernst Eulenburg Ltd

London · Mainz · Madrid · New York · Paris · Prague · Tokyo · Toronto · Zürich

CLAUDE DEBUSSY

Images

1. Gigues   2. Ibéria   3. Rondes de Printemps

The three orchestral *Images*, composed during the years 1906 - 12, are not to be confused with the earlier sets of *Images* for piano solo composed in 1905 and 1907. It seems clear, however, that this third set of *Images* was also originally conceived as piano music; for on 11 September 1905, and again on 29 September the same year, Debussy wrote to his publisher, Jacques Durand, to say that he would very soon have finished 'the three *Images* for two pianos'. Whatever became of this project, it was not until 1908 that *Ibéria*, the first of the set to be composed, was completed in its final orchestral form, to be followed the next year by *Rondes de Printemps* and, three years later, by *Gigues*. The numbering above is the order of publication.

It seems strange that what appears today to be one of Debussy's finest creations should have met with some adverse criticism at the time. He was accused, for example, both of repeating himself and of being too audacious. Each section of *Images* is based on a national musical idiom, English in *Gigues*, Spanish in *Ibéria* and French in the *Rondes*, and this plan disconcerted some musicians and invited criticism. But a good deal of the hostility that the work aroused came from the followers of Vincent d'Indy, nurtured in the austere *Schola Cantorum* of which d'Indy was then the Director and moving spirit. Debussy, however, was warmly supported by the majority of his fellow-composers, including Manuel de Falla (who praised especially the authentic "Hispanism" of *Ibéria*, and Ravel, supposedly his rival, who wrote articles defending Debussy against his detractors.

Images was the last of Debussy's purely orchestral works (*Jeux* was composed for a ballet), and is one of the finest examples of his unrivalled mastery of the art of instrumentation, not to mention its other qualities of fantasy and imagination.

Ibéria

No one familiar with French music can fail to have been struck by the tendency on the part of so many nineteenth and twentieth century composers to borrow from beyond the Pyrenees new rhythms and fresh colours with which to enrich their palette. One has only to think of Bizet, Lalo, Chabrier, Ravel and Debussy himself to realize with what apparent ease these composers acquired a mastery of the Spanish idiom that often seems no less authentic than that of the Spanish musicians themselves. Ravel and Debussy in particular both left more than one masterpiece in the Spanish style. Manuel de Falla said of Debussy's *Soirées dans Grenade* for piano (1903) that 'the entire piece down to the smallest detail makes one feel the character of Spain'. But Debussy's greatest achievement in this field was undoubtedly the orchestral *Image* to which he gave the name *Ibéria*.

The piece is divided into three parts forming a kind of minature symphonic poem, and the composer seems to have distilled into them the very essence of that image of Spain which every Northerner carries in his heart — a land of violent extremes, both of mood and climate, but where everything is enveloped in a sensuous atmosphere of vivid light and colour.

In the first section, *Par les rues et par les chemins* (In the highways and byways), all the glitter and bustle of the streets and the fervour and langour of the characteristic Spanish dance rhythms are vividly depicted. Pizzicato strings, the clattering of castanets and the tambourine's rhythmic rattle all combine to create a highly-coloured picture. Fragments of melody are tossed from one group of instruments to another; excitement and tension increase, and then gradually the atmosphere becomes more rarified and the movement is brought to a wonderfully hushed close — three reiterated notes *pianissimo* on the harp, plucked strings and castanets; a murmur from two clarinets; a flick of the tambourine; an almost inaudible drum-tap; and then silence.

In Part II, *Les parfums de la nuit* (Night scents), the mood changes to one of nocturnal reverie in which the characteristic Habañera rhythm, with its syncopated lilt, casts an almost hypnotic spell.

The transition to Part III, *Le matin d'un jour de fête* (A holiday morning), which follows without a break, is effected by a subtle enharmonic change. This last movement is directed to be played 'in the rhythm of a gay and lively March, heard in the distance.' Soon festivities are in full swing, with chiming bells and twanging guitars; at figs. 56 and 64 the violins are directed to play 'quasi guitara' with their instruments under their arms. After some diversionary interludes in one of which a solo violin, solo oboe and cor anglais take part the March builds up to a triumphant climax.

It is interesting to note that, in a letter to his friend Andre Caplet written while *Ibéria* was being rehearsed, Debussy refers expressly to the way in which the lead into the last movement is managed so naturally that 'it doesn't sound as if it has been written down' ('*Ça n'a pas l'air d'être écrit . . .*'). This, coming from Debussy, was high praise, for we know that he always wanted his music to sound like an improvisation, showing as few signs as possible of that consummate craftsmanship, which he always wanted to conceal.

Ibéria was performed for the first time on 2 February, 1910, at a 'Concert Colonne', conducted by Gabriel Pierné.

Rollo Myers

This edition is taken from the original Durand score with reference to the orchestral parts. The names of the instruments have been put into Italian, as have directions like *sur le chevalet (sul ponticello)*; Debussy himself was inconsistent in this respect, sometimes preferring Italian for such directions as *arco* and *tutti*. Tempo and expression marks have all been left in French, as also his individual instructions about mutes. Inconsistencies of notation have been rationalised and a few errors corrected.

Debussy notated the contrafagotto part 'loco' in both *Ibéria* and *Rondes de Printemps*, probably as a result of studying the full score of Wagner's *Parsifal*. But in *Gigues* the part is more correctly notated an octave above the sound, and the other two *Images* have been brought into line in this respect. Also in accordance with modern practice, horn parts in the bass clef have been altered so that they transpose down, and not up.

D : Durand full score
OP : Orchestra parts

I

41	Tr/Tbni: Accents have been moved from n1 to n2, as in Tuba part and as in 43.
54	Vc/Cb: Confusion between *pizz* and *arco*. D shows Vc *pizz* from 44 to 61, and Cb I from 47 to 83 — where it *must* be *arco* though not so marked. OP shows both parts *arco* 2 quavers before fig. 6, which seems right though this presumably makes it necessary to add *pizz* to Vc I in 57, to Vc II in 61, and to Cb in 62.
93	Vl I¹: D has n2-3 staccato, but there is no staccato in the other string parts.
118	Confusion between *pizz* and *arco*. D has Vla & Cb *pizz* and Vc *arco*: OP have Vla *pizz*, Vc & Cb *arco*. But in the parallel bar, 110, all three parts are *pizz*, and this has been taken as Debussy's intention here even though it necessitates editorial adjustment in 120.
122-78	Cor/Tr: Confusion about mutes. Cor II & IV appear to be unmuted throughout, Tr. muted throughout. Debussy wanted Cor I & III muted for their phrases starting in 138 and 132 respectively, but they cannot be muted by 178 and it is not clear where the mutes are to be removed; perhaps after 140 for Cor I? In practice the players usually handstop up to 177. In OP the trumpets unmute in 178, but D omits the direction.
156	Vla: D has n1-3 in the rhythm of n1-3 in 155, but Vl II suggests that the rhythm of 154 was intended. Perhaps 157 should also have this rhythm, which is invariable before the *pizz* chord in the following bars and makes this chord easier to play.
168	Cor III: D & OP put a cross or 'cuivre' above this note, but it looks like a mistake and it has been omitted. There is no cuivre in the corresponding bar, 172.

181-2 Cor III-IV: D has superfluous ties.

184 Cor: D has a crescendo symbol (leading to p) under both staves, but the diminuendo in the trumpet parts suggest that this is a mistake.

186-202 Vc II/Cb: It looks as though both should be *pizz* or both *acro* from their similar appearance but it is not clear which is intended.

At first *arco* is superfluous for Vc I in 186 it has been taken as applying to all the cellos, and the Cb part has been marked *arco* editorially. (The latter *must* be *arco* by 202.) But it is possible that Vc II remains *pizz* until fig. 21.

206 Tr I: phrasing has been added as in 210.

212 C. ing: n1 omitted in D.

227 VII^2: D has n1 a simple quaver marked p, but see 226 and 230-1.

254 Ob: D unclear as to whether this is 'a 2' or not; OP shows that only one oboe plays.

258-61 Tr II: D ties n1-2 but not the similar notes for Tr 1; the ties seem meaningless and have been omitted.

313 Arpe: D has 'a 2' here, but OP shows that both harps have been playing since 294.

324 Fl. 1: n5 should perhaps be D flat as in 320.

II

11-12 Vl I I^2 should probably be slurred like Vl II.

87 Vl I: D & OP both give the lowest n3 as D harp, but C sharp was clearly intended on both staves.

88-91 Vl I: Neither D or OP makes it clear how many players are required on each stave. Perhaps the last quaver of 87 should be marked 'Tutti a 2', but it is more likely that 6 Soli (desks 1-3) play the top stave and 6 Soli (desks 4-6) and the bottom stave.

102 Tbni: errors in OP resulted from the three parts being crammed on one stave in D; the middle notes were omitted and Tbni II & III both given the bottom line. D is wrong too, with a superfluous slur and dot at the start of the bar and a misleading '2' below the bottom line.

104-8 Vl I: 6 Soli have been playing each stave since 98, and OP has them continuing to do so until 108. D has 6 players to each part in 104 but only 6 in all – 3 to each part – from 106 (as in the parallel bars 77-8). This has been accepted here, but Debussy may have meant the reduction to start in 104.

126-7 Fg I: D ends the phrase on n1 of 126; no doubt Debussy originally thought the bassoon could not continue to double Fl I & Cl I because the D sharp was unplayable. However he must later have found a player who could manage it, for OP gives the whole phrase as in this score. It is always played today.

III

2-4 Vc II: perhaps the *tenuti* and *staccato* dots should be reversed, as in 8-10.

15-18 Cor I - III have been muted since the previous movement; it is probable but not certain that Cor IV should be muted at 18.

45 Confusion between *pizz* and *arco*. Vc I & Cb must be *pizz* though not so shown in D. Vla II, *acro* from 38, is presumably *pizz* at 49, as are all the other strings except for Vl. I.

48 Vl I : D has staccato dots only on the lower stave (not on the last 3 notes); they must be intended on both staves

59 Tr I: D has n4 E flat, OP has C flat, and this is supported by the parallel passage in the second movement (bar 63).

81 Vl I I^2 : D has n2 doubling Vl I I^1 on E, but it should surely be another C sharp as in 80.

83 All naturals before the last quaver are editorial.

117 Both D & OP show Picc 2 entering here, but three notes earlier would make better sense.

I would like to thank Norman Del Mar for valuable help in preparing this edition and these notes.

Roger Fiske

CLAUDE DEBUSSY

Images

1. Gigues   2. Ibéria   3. Rondes de Printemps

Les trois *Images* pour orchestre, composées entre 1906 et 1912, ne doivent pas être confondues avec les deux recueils pour piano parus sous le même titre en 1905 et 1907. Il paraît, cependant, que ce troisième recueil a été, lui aussi, conçu à l'origine pour le piano, car dans une lettre à son éditeur, Jacques Durand, en date du 29 septembre 1905, Debussy écrit: "Et maintenant je vais terminer le plus rapidement possible les *Images* à deux pianos." On ignore ce qu'est devenu ce projet, maid de toute façon ce n'est qu'en 1908 qu'est parue, sous sa forme orchestrale définitive, la première de ces trois *Images*, *Ibéria*, suivie un an plus tard par *Rondes de Printemps*, et trois ans plus tard par *Gigues*. Les numéros ci-dessus indiquent l'ordre de leur publication.

Que cette oeuvre de Debussy, que nous considérons aujourd'hui comme une de ses plus belles créations, ait suscité dans certains milieux des critiques déavorables peut nous paraître assez invraisemblable. On reprochait par exemple au compositeur d'être trop audacieux et, en même temps, de n'avoir rien de nouveau à dire. Il est vrai que le plan de l'ouvrage (chacun des trois morceaux dont se composent *Images* est inspiré par un chant populaire national — anglais dans *Gigues* espagnol dans *Ibéria* et français dans *Rondes de Printemps*) était fait pour dérouter quelque peu les musiciens comme les critiques; mais il est probable que c'est surtout par les disciples de Vincent d'Indy, partisans de l'école franckiste, que l'oeuvre fut mal jugée. Néanmoins, Debussy pouvait compter sur l'appui de la plupart de ses confrères, notamment Manuel de Falla (qui louait "l'hispanisme" authentique d'*Ibéria*), et Maurice Ravel (qui passait pour son rival). Ce dernier, en effet, écrivit des articles pour défendre Debussy contre ses détracteurs.

Images fut la dernière des oeuvres purement symphoniques de Debussy (*Jeux* fut composé pour un ballet), et peut être considérée comme un des plus beaux exemples de sa maîtrise incontestée dans l'art de l'orchestration, sans parler des autres richesses d'esprit et d'imagination qu'elle recèle.

Ibéria

Aucun connaisseur de la musique française ne peut manquer d'être frappé par la tendance de tant de compositeurs des dix neuvième et vingtième siècles à emprunter d'au-delà des Pyrénées des rythmes nouveaux et des couleurs fraîches dont ils enrichissent leur palette. Qu'on pense seulement à Bizet, Lalo, Chabrier, Ravel et surtout Debussy, l'on constatera avec facilité apparente ces compositeurs se sont approprié le langage musical spécifique de l'Espagne, au point qu'il ne semble pas, dans leur oeuvre, moins authentique que celui des musiciens espagnols eux-mêmes. Ravel et Debussy, en particulier, ont laissé, tous deux, plus d'un chef-d'oeuvre dans le style espagnol; et c'est à propos des *Soirées dans Grenade* pour piano (1903) de Debussy que Manuel de Falla disait que 'le morceau entier, jusqu'au plus petit détail, vous fait sentir le génie de l'Espagne.' Pourtant, ce que Debussy a fait de meilleur dans ce domaine est incontestablement l'*Image* orchestrale qu'il intitula *Iberia*.

Le morceau se compose de trois parties qui forment une sorte de poème symphonique en miniature où l'image de l'Espagne, que porte en son coeur tout habitant de Nord, est évoquée sous tous ses aspects divers: celle d'une terre de violents contrastes, mais où tout s'enveloppe d'une atmosphère sensuelle de lumière crue et de couleurs vives.

La première section, *Par les rues et par les chemins*, dépeint vivement le scintillement et la remue-ménage des rues, avec toute la ferveur et la langueur des rythmes de danse propres à l'Espagne. Le bruissement des cordes le claquement des castagnettes, le rythme des tambourins se fondent en un tableau haut en couleurs.

Des fragments de mélodie rebondissent d'un groupe d'instruments à l'autre; l'excitation et la tension vont augmentant jusqu'à ce que peu à peu tout s'apaise, et le morceau se termine en toute tranquillité: trois notes *pianissimo* répétées (harpe, violons et castagnettes); le murmure de deux clarinettes; le tambourin qu'on effleure; le battement presque inaudible d'un tambour-puis le silence.

Dans la seconde partie, *Les parfums de la nuit* où l'agitation cède a la rêverie nocturne, le rythme typique d'habanera, avec sa cadence syncopée, exerce un charme presque hallucinant.

La transition vers la troisième partie, *Le matin d'un jour de fête*, qui suit sans interruption, se fait par une subtile modulation enharmonique qui introduit la dernière partie, laquelle doit être jouée 'dans un rythme de marche lointaine, alerte et joueuse'. Bientôt la fête bat son plein, les guitares vibrent (à certains endroits les violons jouent 'quasi guitara", avec leurs instruments sous le bras – voir aux mesures 00 et 00); les cloches carillonnent. Après quelques interludes qui font diversion – dans l'un d'eux on n'entend qu' un violon, un hautbois et un cor anglais – la marche poursuit son chemin vertigineux pour finir dans un éclat triomphal.

Il est intéressant de noter que Debussy, écrivant à son ami André Caplet alors qu'on répétait *Iberia*, lui signale 'combien l'enchaînement des 'parfums de la nuit' avec 'le matin d'un jour de fête' se fait si naturellement que *ca n'a pas l'air d'etre ecrit . . .*' C'est là, du point de vue de Debussy, le plus grande éloge, car nous savons qu'il a toujours voulu que sa musique ait l'air improvisé et trahisse aussi peu que possible le métier parfait qu'il avait toujours soin de cacher.

Iberia fut joué pour la première fois lors d'un Concert Colonne, sous la direction de Gabriele Pierné, le 2 fevrier, 1910.

Rollo Myers

Cette édition est tirée de la partition originale Durand, avec renvoi aux parties d'orchestre. Nous avons traduit en Italien les noms des instruments ainsi que les indications comme "sur le chevalet" (Sul ponticello)   Debussy lui-même manqua de conséquence à cet égard, préférant parfois l'Italien pour des directives comme, par exemple, *arco* et *tutti*. Nous laissons en Français toutes le indications de mouvement et d'expression, ainsi que ses directives particulières sur les sourdines. Nous avons rendu uniformes les inconséquences dans la notation, et nous avons corrigé quelques erreurs.

C'est peut-être à la suite d'une étude de la partition complète du *Parsifal* de Wagner que Debussy a écrit "loco" pour la partie de contre-basson dans *Ibéria* et dans les *Rondes de Printemps*. Dans *Gigues*, par contre, cette partie est plus correctement notés une octave au-dessus des sons réels, et nous y avons conformé sous ce rapport les deux autres *Images*. De même, suivant la pratique moderne, les parties de cor dans la clef de fa ont été modifiées pour faciliter des transpositions descendantes et non ascendantes.

CLAUDE DEBUSSY

Images

1. Gigues   2. Ibéria   3. Rondes de Printemps

Die drei *Images* für Orchester, die Debussy zwischen 1906 und 1912 komponierte, haben nichts mit den *Images* für Klavier gemein, die er in den Jahren 1905 und 1907 schrieb. Dennoch scheint es, dass auch dieses dritte, *Images* betitelte Werk, zunächst für Klavier gedacht war. Debussy schrieb nämlich am 11. September 1905 und wiederum am 29. September des gleichen Jahres an seinen Verleger Jacques Durand, dass die drei *Images* für zwei Klaviere' bald fertig wären. Wann, und weshalb dieser ursprüngliche Plan aufgegeben wurde, ist nicht zu ermitteln, jedenfalls wurde *Ibéria*, das zuerst geschriebene dieser drei *Images*, erst im Jahre 1908 in seiner endgültigen Form für Orchester vollendet. Im nächsten Jahr folgten die *Rondes de Printemps*, und endlich, drei Jahre später, *Gigues*. Die Stücke wurden in der oben angegebenen Reihenfolge veröffentlicht.

Es scheint uns heute verwunderlich, dass eines der bedeutendsten Werke Debussys zunächst nicht allgemein den ihm gebührenden Anklang fand. Einerseits wurde Debussy für seine Kühnheit kritisiert, andererseits wurde ihm vorgeworfen, sich zu wiederholen. Was ferner Kritik hervorrief und einige Musiker als befremdend empfanden, war der Plan, nach dem jedes der drei *Images* in einem für das entsprechende Land typischen musikalischen Idiom geschrieben war: in *Gigues* war das Idiom englisch, spanisch in *Ibéria* und französisch in *Rondes*. Jedoch die hauptsächlichsten Angriffe gegen das Werk rührten von den Anhängern Vincent d'Indy's her, welche die strengen Grundsätze der von d'Indy geleiteten *Schola Cantorum* zu ihren eigenen gemacht hatten. Die Mehrzahl der anderen Komponisten setzte sich allderdings energisch für Debussy ein, wie zum Beispiel Manuel de Falla, der besonders den authentischen Charakter des spanischen Idioms in *Ibéria* rühmte, sowie Ravel (Debussys vermeintlicher Rivale), der den Komponisten in seinen Artikeln gegen unkritische Angreifer verteidigt.

Images war Debussys letztes rein für Orchester geschriebenes Werk (das spätere *Jeux* komponierte er als Balletmusik). Die Partitur ist eines der besten Beispiele von Debussys unübertroffener Instrumentierungskunst, und die Komposition als Ganzes zeichnet sich durch eine Fülle von Ideen und einen unvergleichlichen Reichtum an Phantasie aus.

Ibéria

Es ist auffallend, dass so viele französische Komponisten des neunzehnten und zwanzigsten Jahrhunderts dazu neigten, das Tonbild ihrer Partituren durch neue Rhythmen und starke Klangfarben von jenseits der Pyrenäen zu beleben. Erwähnen wir nur Bizet, Lalo, Chabrier, Ravel und Debussy, die alle das musikalische Idiom Spaniens meisterhaft beherrschten — so meisterhaft in der Tat, dass ihre spanische Musik nicht weniger authentisch klang als die der spanischen Komponisten. Besonders waren es Debussy und Ravel, die mehr als ein Meisterwerk im spanischen Stil komponierten. Manuel de Falla sagte über Debussys *Soires dans Grenade* (1903), dass das ganze Stück bis ins letzte dem Hörer das Wesen Spaniens vermittelt'. Unter Debussys Kompositionen im spanischen Stil war jedoch ohne Zweifel das zweite der *Images* für Orchester, *Iberia*, sein Meisterwerk.

Iberia besteht aus drei Teilen, die zusammen gewissermassen eine sinfonische Dichtung in Miniatur ergeben. Es ist dem Komponisten anscheinend gelungen, jenes Bild Spaniens, das die Bewohner der nördlichen Länder im Herzen tragen, im Wesentlichen in seiner Musik auszudrücken: das Bild eines Landes grosser Gegensätze, sowohl in der Stimmung wie auch im Klima, wo aber alles von hellem Licht und starken Farben umgeben ist.

Die Musik des ersten Teils, *Par les rues et par les chemins* (Auf Strassen und Wegen), beschreibt den Glanz und das lebhafte Treiben in den Strassen Spaniens, sowie die Leidenschaft und Sehnsucht, die in den spanischen Tanzrhythmen zum Ausdruck kommt. Das Pizzicato der Streicher, das Klappern der Kastagnetten und das rhythmische Gerassel des Tamburins tragen ihren Teil zu dem in starken Farben gemalten Tonbild bei. Fragmente von Themen werden von den verschiedenen Gruppen der Instrumente aufgegriffen; Aufregung und Spannungwachsen, bis endlich die Stimmung ruhiger wird, und der Satz in einer wundervollen Stille verklingt — mit drei *pianissimo* wiederholten Noten auf der Harfe, mit dem

Pizzicato der Streicher und den Kastagnetten, dem Geflüster von zwei Klarinetten, einem Anschlag des Tamburins und einem fast unhörbaren Trommelschlag.

Der zweite Teil trägt den Titel *Les parfums de la nuit* (Düfte der Nacht). Der Charakter der Musik gleicht hier einem träumerischen Nachtstück. Der typische Habanera-rhythmus mit seinen schwingenden Synkopen hält den hörer in seinem Bann.

Die Überleitung zum dritten Teil, *Le matin d'un jour de fete* (Festmorgen), der ohne Unterbrechung folgt, beruht auf einer subtilen enharmonischen Verwechslung. Dieser letzte Satz soll laut Vorschrift im Rhythmus eines lustigen, lebhaften, aus der Ferne gehörten Marsches' gespielt werden. Bald sind die Festlichkeiten in vollem Gang, mit klingenden Glocken und gezupften Guitarren. In den Takten 000 und 000 werden die Geigenspieler angewiesen, ihre Instrumente quasi guitara', unter dem Arm gehalten, zu spielen. Nach verschiedenen Episoden, deren eine sich durch die Verwendung von Solovioline, Solo-oboe und Englischhorn auszeichnet, erreicht der marsch seinen triumphalen Höhepunkt.

Interessant ist ein Brief, den Debussy während einer Probe von *Iberia* an seinen Freund Andr Caplet schrieb, in dem er ausdrücklich darauf hinwies, dass der Übergang zum letzten Satz so klänge und sich so natürlich vollsöge, als wäre er gar nicht aufgeschrieben worden' (*Ca n'a pas l'air d'etre ecrit . . .*). Ein solches Urteil Debussys muss als grosses Lob angesehen werden, denn er strebte stets danach, seinen Kompositionene den Charakter von Improvisationen zu geben und so wenig wie möglich von seinem aussergewöhnlichen technischen Können spüren zu lassen.

Iberia wurde am 2. Februar 1910 in einem *Concert Colonne* unter der Leitung von Gabriel Picrn uraufgeführt.

Rollo Myers
Deutsche Übersetzung Stefan de Haan

Diese Ausgabe beruht auf der von Durand verlegten Originalpartitur, mit Bezugnahme auf die Orchesterstimmen. Die Bezeichnung der Instrumente, sowie Hinweise wie „*Sur le chevalet*" *(sul ponticello)* ins Italienische übersetzt. Debussy war selbst in dieser Hinsicht inkonsequent, da er zuweilen italienische Ausdrücke, wie „*arco*" und „*tutti*", vorzog. Alle Tempo- und Ausdrucksbezeichnungen sind wie im Original französisch.* Uneinheitlichkeiten in der Notierung sind in Übereinstimmung gebracht, und einige Fehler korrigiert worden.

Debussy notierte das Kontrafagott in *Iberia* und *Rondes de Printemps*, vielleicht zufolge seines Studiums der Partitur von Wagners, *Parsifal*, „loco". Da jedoch die Stimme in *Gigues* korrekterweise eine Oktave höher notiert ist als sie klingt, wurden die beiden anderen *Images* damit in Übereinstimmung gebracht. Auch sind die Hörner, soweit sie im Bass-Schlüssel stehen, so umgeschrieben worden, dass sie wie heute üblich, nach unten, und nicht nach oben, transponieren.

*wie auch seine Hinweise über Dämpfer

Ibéria
I. Par les rues et par les chemins

Claude Debussy
1862–1918

Edited by Roger Fiske

4

6

20

EE6603

44

EE6603

45

EE 6603

51

EE 6603

II. Les parfums de la nuit

55

F.F. 6603

64

EE 6603

84
a tempo (En animant)
47
2 Fl.
2 Ob.
Cl. (A) I/II
Fg. I/II
III
Cfg.
Cor. (F) I/II
III/IV
Arpa I
Vl. I
Vl. II
Vla.
Vc.
4 Cb.
p soutenu
soutenu et expressif
solo ôtez la Sourdine
6 soli
unis.
tutte a 2
p souple
cresc.

77

EE 6603

78

EE6603

III. Le matin d'un jour de fête

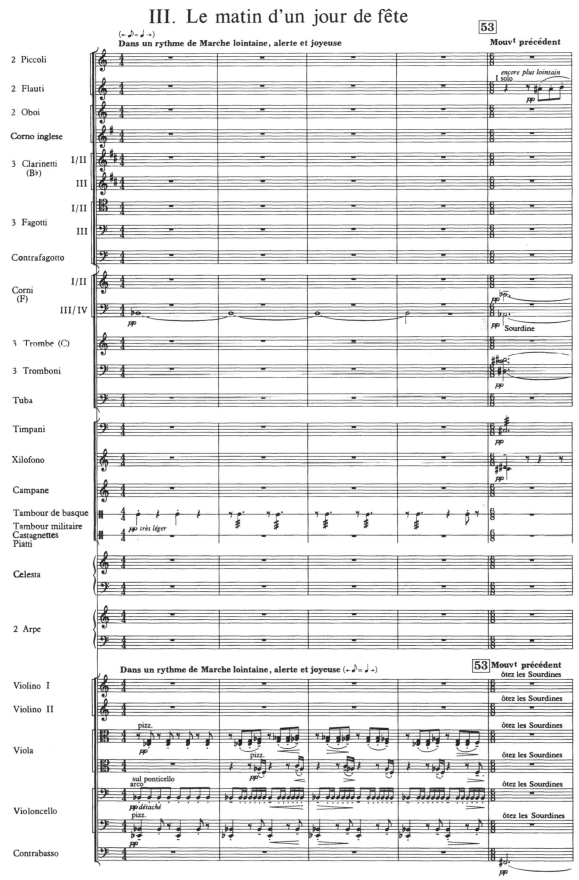

99

EE 6603